Start Again

Miriam Sagan

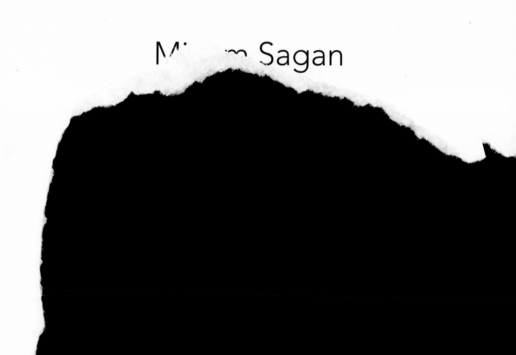

Some of these poems first appeared in: *Agony Opera, Ashley O'melia blog, Areogram, Beliveau Review, Buddhist Poetry Review, Chaotic Merge, Dipak Girl, Muddy River Poetry Review, Pasatiempo/Santa Fe New Mexican, Poemic, Scissorstail,* and *Witches and Pagans*

ISBN 978-1-952204-24-1

Printed in the United States of America

Start Again

Contents

ALONG THE CHAMA

I greet everyone I meet
on the river path

the fisherman in his red shirt
his old wife with the little dog

"cute dog," I say
waiting for her smile

out towards the Brazos cliffs
it's raining

mist like a Chinese painting
and huge stone calving out of the mountain range

a partial but sincere rainbow
appearing and disappearing

and the "check tire pressure" light comes on
and we turn back

the air machine is on the blink
because "it was hit by lightning"

the convenience store clerk won't make change
until I pull my grandmother-in-trouble face

really, the tires are fine, just a little low
not flat

it's dark now, and I don't know
which neon sign is prettier

VACANCY or
NO VACANCY.

THE MAGICIAN

for my mother's 80th birthday
in the nice restaurant
overlooking the river

my father has hired
a highly rated
magician

to entertain us
at lunch
but the magician is creepy

doesn't seem
to realize
the children have grown

to teenagers
who now
openly mock him

then run off
to weep
and smoke in the bathroom

no bouquet
of paper flowers
pulled from your ear

can cure time
and its progression
to the old woman

my mother must become
and then the still older woman
who has forgotten her own name

magic is everywhere
my father the alchemist
turns

someone who loved him—
me—
into someone who left.

In the Monastery of a Nice Day to Start Again

as if the sea rose
came up the two
front steps
covered the mat
foamed at the front door

sleep deposited its cargoes
love also
ebbed and flowed
set my naked body
next to yours
as I pillowed your head
beneath my chin

I danced
watching the mountains
to to the west
Billy Idol
belting
I danced
my crippled girl
and my other self
together

the mountain was not
just watching
it was dancing too
only its movements in time
imperceptible.

Ranchos de Taos

you think you
have problems…
windchimes
kept us awake
all night
along with the neighbor's
barking dog
and the dance music
turned up loud
not to mention
the moon…

magpie feathers float on the air
something
killed and ate
a bird;
a cauldron, a metal rabbit, a lantern
guard the storeroom
of a different feeling

Taos Mountain is still
snow-covered,
the day after Easter
I'd be careful,
breeze ruffles the pages of a book
about grenades and the Chinese revolution

the tiny girl
like a crow
can count
at least up to five
for how mysterious
the hacienda is
that always
has one more bed
than the number
of residents.

ORANGE PEEL

in a black pottery
bowl

what will you
pray for
today?

in Ranchos de Taos
doves fly
out of the church towers

no one needs
to ask them
to return

they will do that
anyway.

TIAMAT IN NETS

1.

my daughter
in a black silk robe
kimono
    falling open
while her baby crawls naked
trying to climb up
and stand

outside, the big wind knocks
against the house
like a bandit
out of basin land west of the Pecos

in the snow, the peacock
has flown into a pine tree
next to my daughter's chicken coop

all this

2.

a stranger
electric blue
appears on this side
of the river

you've camped alone

trees seared by fire
some years ago
stand skeletal
although meadow
has mostly
reappeared
on charred soil

to the west
old volcanoes
capped in snow
characteristic shape
of something
that has blown its top

nuclear reactor
melting down
glows—and those who lived
say it was
beautiful

you cross the Jabbok river
branched
like the Rio Grande
pebbled wash
waterway
in a dry place
given to disruption

by now
it must be night
that stranger
appears again—
after all
isn't this a true
story

blue
is the opposite
of red
sky gods
may have skin
the color of the sky
cerulean
might be only
watercolor

turns out, you also
want something
from this wingless
traveler

sea green
papyrus stalk hieroglyph
impossible and lovely dye
those who mix
blue and yellow
exiled

made in G-d's image
why shouldn't we
stroke the palette
turn the color wheel
and pinning down
the naked angel
ask its name.

3.

who invented
the outline
30,000 years ago

smoking mirror
might show
what? the face

of the deep?
the baby entranced
by a spray of mist

coming out of
a humidifier
charmingly shaped like a cloud

I tell her
darling, this is
ephemeral

you can't catch it
or hold it
and the sooner

you realize this
the happier
you will be.

4.

we drive to Taos
across the gorge
where earth splits

and where someone
casually leaning against a railing
might jump

you change your name
as easily
as I change my clothes

one moment your name
is City, and the next
Chaos

and once we saw
the goddess
hanging in a museum

crocheted curtain
creation on a screen
and although

we'd paid our money
for admission
I felt a chill

at what
demands
sacrifice.

5.

in the middle of the night
they told me
to leave the room
where you labored
(so far in vain)

they put a needle
in your lower back, and I
your mother

went to sit
in the chapel, empty and dark

and prayed to barbed wire
the trash that blows
against a fence

March wild
in its rampage

talk about
hieroglyph, Linear B
ideogram

what I don't understand
can never translate

your shriek
as I invoke
a Penitente world

saints of the north
who will listen
although I am a Jew

because
they've heard this before.

6.

I tell you:

Tiamat
got caught
in a net

and you say:

I know who Tiamat is.

THE STAR

west on shabby Agua Fria street
in the solstice dusk
to the village itself
where strands
of blue lights
hang in otherwise
bare trees
and the occasional
solitary star
adorns the roof
of an old lady
whose son-in-law put it up

from this tender portion
of what I call my world
we watch
Saturn and Jupiter
conjunct, appear
as one
while in reality
they are
456 million miles
apart

with you driving
and me
riding shotgun
in the passenger's seat.

The Zen Master

tosses his napkin—
without meaning to
I catch it

passes me an apple
which I eat
including
the core.

Masked strangers
hope
to not infect me

but also
want to rob me
of something

like all
faceless creatures
in all versions of the tale.

You started talking
about fox spirits
out in the misty rice fields
walking at night

I told

you
to be quiet

you only
half-
listened.

Back in the freezing
kitchen
of the Japanese farm house

we boiled the kettle
which did not change shape
into a badger
and run off.

Still, I touch
my own features
in the empty
mirror.

SPOUSES

"What's that noise?" the wife asks the husband
even after so many years

night noises, raccoons, and the federal government
are his problem to solve.

It's not late, before midnight
"Firecrackers?" he speculates

although it sounds like gunshot
and we're just blocks from the capitol building

where armed men
show the threat of force.

But probably the husband is correct,
it's midsummer's night, and America's birthday

a few weeks away
although frankly I'm not sure

this country of mine
deserves much of a party.

Much later, towards the witching hour

skunks head home and spray

through our bathroom window
that opens on the narrow alley

that creatures use to cross.
The thrashers are sleeping

in the blossoming cholla bush,
not once in all these years

has the invisible neighbor's orange cat
manage to catch a bird

in all those cactus needles.

THE FOOL

the baby is naked
I'm clothed
she has the hose
and foolishly I shriek
"don't get me wet!"
egging her on

her blond, tousled hair
bangs in her eyes
she can say "ant" and "please"
but what is she really
thinking?

so too the neighbor's bees
cast runes in the book of the day
purple blossoms
I've cultivated for
pollinators all

in the ruined city
there is honey
beneath the masonry
slabs
(still standing in the desert)

how close, in autumn,
things are
to going
to seed
as am I.

An Odd—Large—Painting

in the rental casita
a plump woman
asleep, on a lumpy sofa
bare feet
on a red pillow
despite the green
ferny wallpaper
this is no
Matisse
her unconvincing
knees
seem faraway
from her head
while her toes
are off the canvas completely

there are days
I've felt like this
no Sleeping Beauty
just trying to get through
a hot afternoon
a third trimester
high school
menopause
too enervated
to even put ice cubes
in a glass of tap water

but this is bought and sold, signed
hanging on the wall
the artist's name
a blur beneath a painted cushion

and the day seems like a to do list
I left for myself
twenty years ago
forgetting to even mention to say
I love you.

THE CHARIOT

anyone can read the stars

earth's fortunes
obscured
by satellites

autumn equinox
a goldfinch hangs
among cowpen daisies

I saw the moon
going down, due west
of my pillow

and golden constellations
on the lapis sky
inside a tomb

you want some advice?
drop the reins
take your hands off the wheel

a many-armed
goddess
might be

disguised as a beggar
in an old cloak
might be

the neighbor
you should love
a little better

than the way—
nagging, imperfect—
you love yourself

might be
the charioteer and you
the passenger

or the reverse
like a horoscope
that could be

anyone's
but still speaks to you.

In the Monastery of a Birdbath Filled with Snow

each garden pot
perfectly rimmed
in temporary
chilly white elegance

the toddler has
scattered a hundred tiny
worry dolls
around the house
(she does this every day)
they are almost featureless
scraps of thread and cloth
size of my fingernail

I keep the world
at a distance—
the width of my small yard
from front door
to mailbox—
history with its tyrants
its homicidal quarrels
in parking lots
its bronze memorials
to a version
I don't want to
read

in the dish drainer
I come upon a child's spoon
clean and ready again
painted with bright hearts—
it was your mother's—
I kept it,
not even knowing
who was arriving
next.

AFLOAT

in the lilac waves
with the silver undertow

in a boat of femurs
the backwashed sea
lit from within
all the drowned

this is no schooner,
smuggler, captain, child
in a tide of backpacks

I'm afloat
on the wooden dinghy
of my story

empty oarlocks
floating oars.

LAKESIDE

at dusk we go down to the lake
come upon a woman bathing
no goddess naked
almost old and plump in two-piece suit
but like the huntress
surrounded by three black dogs
who splash, friendly
if we are

absent-mindedly
you toss a stick
into the water
and one of the Labs
dashes to retrieve it—
we notice how the level
is rising
out of the lake bowl
and starting to flood the shore

I walk over pebbles
look at glacier's detritus
try to draw
the spots and speckles
in my mind's eye
each rock
like a smoothed, dented
fractal of the shoreline

when we turn back
they're gone
back in the truck, no doubt
or maybe just
vanished
into last light
on the lake's surface.

In the Monastery of Circumambulation
and the Statue of Liberty

walking by
what was once
the Hospital
for Crippled Children
I lean on my cane
continue past
Veterans' Memorial Park
where a smallish replica
of the Statue of Liberty
commemorates 9/11
and a replica of the Vietnam wall
reminds us of…
well, things you have not yet
had the privilege
of forgetting

this is
Truth or Consequences
New Mexico
with thorny bushes
and so many
lovely particular
little birds

in an ordinary neighborhood
a whitewashed stupa

trimmed in gold Buddhas
stands positioned
with the Rio Grande to the south
a hill shaped like a turtle—
sporting a water tower
shaped like a water tower—
to the north

I circumambulate
in the wrong direction at first
my brain addled
not by a vow
to save all beings
but by my usual
dyslexia
then switch course
go round three times
clockwise
in the correct manner
and bow
making a gassho
with both hands

my intention?
just to stop quarreling
with all the things
I do not understand.

LADY OF THE HOUSE

my cousin had
a gold watch with diamonds
a tiny lid covered its face
and she kind-heartedly
let us play with it

she had feather-covered mules
for her small feet
and a locket with pictures
of her three children

her husband
had a mistress
or more than one
in the city
maybe a special girl
and a few for a good time

among the so-called
Russian Jews
not every man was faithful
bent over a torah

there were gangsters
and I knew them well

this world

held lavish bowls of fruit
but kindness
was scarcer

I don't know why
my mother's cousin
cared for me and my sisters
taught us to knit
(European style)
but not to cast off

so that our knitting
went on
endlessly.

Parallel Lines

tracks
in the snowy parking lot

rinsing black ink
off the too stiff brush

at sunset, Jemez mountains
disappear

dark, glowing clouds
bring something else

the child begs for salt
then licks it off the oilcloth

only in my dreams
do I touch

deer's velvety antlers
their nibbling mouths

if I knew this was beauty
could I relax once and for all?

or is it my fate
to keep moving…

SWIMMER

Barefoot on the hot cement
between the turquoise pool
and the ice cream stand
my scrawny seven-year-old self
with my small belly
pooched out
above the band of my bathing suit.

Suddenly I'm ringed
by the big kids, much
bigger than I am
mostly boys, one girl,
and they say
"let's throw you
in the pool
and see if you can swim."

I can swim,
I just don't want to be
thrown,
so I smile back
and mouth off
and say—"sure,
you can easily
toss me in
I'd never fight you
I'd never win."

And for some
miraculous reason
this makes them laugh
and walk away.

No longer threatened
I just jump in myself
chlorine stinging my eyes
water up my nose
and do the dead man's float,
beneath the rippled surface,
the legs of other swimmers,
I see the city
I've always known was there,
of coral towers
with pearl windows
house of peacock shimmer
abalone
with roof of oyster shell
shingles.

It rises from the painted
bottom of the pool,
I'm careful
not to cut my foot
on its pagodas
as I dive deeper down,
then surface
holding a penny
plucked from the drain.

In the Monastery of My Opinions and Some Birds

today
I heard people say
a few stupid things
about poetry
and even stupider things
about war

as I was loading the car
to go south
I heard three crows
in a leafless tree
chatting
about how
they once
were dinosaurs

coyote
follows three people—I mean
three sandhill cranes—
at a respectful
distance
they won't make dinner
as they walk along the corn field
ungainly
in their wings

until perfect, they take

to the currents
of the air
above the bosque
with its red salt cedar
its black ducks
its water thrown
hallucinogenic blue
like silk before the feet
of bare desert mountains

the daytime moon
is waxing
just not that quickly
my thoughts seem suspended
intimate with stories
of the past
and unborn stories
still to come
while a huge, buzzing flock
of blackbirds wheels
as if to illustrate
classic swarm theory
until they turn
against the light
vanish.

PULL

I pull the baby
in a blue plastic car
along the empty dirt road
beneath the inverted
basin of a sky

two things are blue—
one small
one enormous

the baby has a fate
I can't read
she likes to open
a board book
then
put it in her mouth

the world has
gone to hell
and left us here
like shells
tossed up by a storm
to litter the tide's wrack line

a pair of unmatched, ridged
bivalvular
angel wings

one big
one little.

Obelisk

October snow
on the yellow
cottonwood leaves

the last
of my old poets
is dead

in the dry capital
of what once
was Mexico

on the plaza
an obelisk
to the Union dead

and to the Indian wars
with its racist epithet
has been pulled down

Kit Carson—
that Judas—
is next

his monument
outside the federal building
plastered with a warning sign

some say a marshal
sits day and night
guarding it

but I think
he is
a ghost

the baby's pink sneaker
falls off in the snow
wet and solitary

when I retrieve it
it won't fit
much longer.

YOU AND I TOGETHER

the morning star shone behind the paper shade
squash blossoms emerged from darkness
huge, prickly leaves, umbrellas that welcomed rain
I didn't realize there'd be so many needles

I'm no hermit, you're sleeping here beside me
an old man and an old woman breathing the same air
it's possible the image is esoteric
mostly I just want to say I'm here.

MANHATTAN

My father called everyone "Sir."
It was his egalitarian mission,
they called him that, he responded in kind.
My father was not naturally
a lover of people
but he loved humanity
in general. SIR
he'd bellow
at the man selling chestnuts
from a cart—hot
they burned through mittens
as we tossed them
from hand to hand
before peeling, finally eating them,
so meaty and sweet.

My childhood is gone
now from that ravaged city
where piled corpses
are buried on the little islands
that welcomed them before—
unmarked, nameless.

The chalk
erased from the sidewalk
the hopscotch labyrinth
that once led—
throw a stone, then hop hop—
to the square marked
Paradise.

IN THE MONASTERY OF MARGARITAS AND THREE VISIBLE
PLANETS

Mars, then
Jupiter and Saturn
conjunct
growing closer

the velvety evening dress blue of the sky

two kids
by the trestle
one bicycle on the tracks
no train will
ever pass by
let alone
stop

one of them
turns to go
walking home alone
in the dark

we discuss
how all the visible
planets
are currently visible
(by eye, or telescope)
and I say—
but not
the invisible ones

like wow,
you say

I think we might be
getting on each other's
nerves
just a little

but I embrace your back
in the cold
hold tight.

ANCESTORS

zodiac swam in its round
above the wooden ark
veiled women hid behind
a mechitza of water and blood
if I was a child
I ran among their legs
if I was a child I ran

in the Red Cafe in Kiev
at the teetering round table
in steam and smoke like a railway station
tea served in endless glasses
they are shouting again
those philosophers
too broke to pay
but suddenly I can't hear them
sound fades, they're ghosts
and what am I?

in all of history, who can care
about one girl, tired, besmirched
sitting by the coals of a dying fire
who can care
about birch trees—
there are so many…

who can care about rape
about how my eyes turn
a betraying green
or how my fingers curl helplessly
as DNA deforms my hand
the double helix of Vikings, Cossacks, the Rus
come down out of the cold, shamanic north
for bad, for worse

ancestors come if I call
smelling like a snuffed candle
and come if I don't call
smelling of hospital corridors and panic
for the angels are too busy
encouraging each blade of grass to grow
reciting the alphabet
but only from aleph to aleph
they have not yet
reached the first letter
of my name

before this, a wall
before that, destruction
before that, an ark on the deep
a raven, a dove, an opinion
about what survives.

OFFSPRING

you look like me
we sit at the square table
our DNA walked out of Africa
into the Iberian peninsula

indigo pattern
circles, dots
lit candles
we covered our hair with lacy shawls

sat in cafes
Kiev, Avenue B
in the bars
of places called "Old Town"

and so we attempted
to avoid
subjugation—
a word, a coin, a slap

the "Thank G-d
for not having made me
a woman"
a man prays every morning

sitting cross-legged,
daughter,
smoking on the curb—
refuse to say amen.

BENEATH THE SUN

even in the womb you dreamed
of a field of yellow flowers

you heard our voices
and thought we were crows perched
on a broken-down corral

you held my gaze
and saw ghosts and static and the insides
of cat ears

you tried to turn over
but you didn't know
what "over" meant

God felt new and fresh
in your tiny fist
your sucking mouth

you heard us laugh
and thought the wind
had come down the chimney

the biggest dog
licked your toes—
you thought it was the rising tide
of an inland sea

you dreamed
about yellow flowers
without knowing "yellow"

you crossed a field
an enormous one

bigger than the universe
or our hope, our expectation,

to arrive here.

City of the Holy Faith

snow in the mountains
the capital city
nestled at the foot
of the Sangre de Cristo mountains

suddenly smaller
more intimate
as it was when I first
came to town

out of the gray
western sky
a medevac
helicopter appears

carrying God knows who
to God knows where.

A NORTH KOREAN MISSILE

flashes across
the Sea of Japan

we miss the news
don't even know
to worry—
preoccupied climbing a small mountainside
up the path of Inari shrines

a long line of red Shinto gates
and tiny ones
the size of a shoe box
ceramic fox figurines
pine trees, clear sky

I'm not praying
for anything in particular
too old
to have to pass an important examination
and content enough—
after all
we've brought a bag of cherries
spit out the pits

but maybe my daughter
was praying
to get the child
she got

and maybe I was praying
to stop taking each day
like a test.

Dawn Struck

Dawn struck the mountain
I needed to awaken

back into my
old crippled self

don't tell me
what word to use

after all, who really knows
the tree's name except the tree

I opened the door of the one-room house
stuffy with a night of dreams

stacked up like airplanes
in fog over a great city

the toddler pulls my turquoise skirt
to lead me

she wants to go in
she wants to go out

the metal Buddha
cast from the emptiness of a mold

when I was young
I thought I'd leave this world of forms

now I see
a bird on a waving branch

throw a shadow
on the whitewashed wall.

BY THE SHRINE

tree with roots
in the heavens
upside-down
reflection
twin to the giant gnarled one
in the temple grounds

ancient as a shark, moss, diatom

brew the fan-shaped leaves
drink a tea to stay awake
memorizing the sutras

yellow flutters and falls
on stone steps

neither Buddha nor Shinto

gingko.

THE DEVIL

a truckful of saints
going in the opposite direction
from us

seems a sign
the bed full of
plaster St. Francises

and so many Virgins
of Guadalupe
each with her halo

and her foot
firmly
on the Aztecan serpent

here at the intersection
of Atoll Bikini
heading towards

Trinity and Oppenheimer
then going south
past the pueblo casinos

where the great seal
notes the date
of the Pueblo Revolt

and the motto of Los Alamos
is "Where Discoveries
are Made"

so bland and in
the passive voice
instead of
"This is Where
What We Call History
Ended."

MIDRASH

In the middle of the night
I couldn't tell the difference

between what I wanted
and what I had

between my first
and my second husband

between what I loved
and what loved me.

The neighbor keeps a light on
against burglars

although he no longer stands smoking
and his mother is long dead

behind his house
a recluse prays

in front of mine
four brothers shoot hoops

in the middle of the night
a coyote strolls across St. Francis Drive

Coyote pretends to sleep on a park bench
counting stars

I say: you can count on me
even, if in darkness,

I can't tell
the difference

between Rachel and Leah
Jacob and the angel.

OJO CALIENTE

Once, between here and there
I left a copy

of Le Guin's "The Left Hand of Darkness"
in an unmade bed

on an old hotel room
at a hot spring

south of Tres Piedras
and north of Hernandez.

It wasn't so long ago
that you had to bear right

at the round, abandoned adobe
and take the one-lane bridge

through the pueblo.
But it was longer ago

that you could soak in the pools
and a private bathtub

and get wrapped in towel and blankets
for under $7.00.

The first time I was here
was in the 1970s

on the women's side
when I was in love

with someone
who would never love me back.

And yes, I bought another copy
of the book. And finished it.

BAROQUE

yellow leaves
on the cooling wind
the day was exoteric

and I could read
my own mood
reflected in your familiar face

but not everything
even this side of the veil
is seen

the plastic chair
at the archeological dig
might outlast the tomb

false door in the Egyptian wall
is a real door
to the land of the dead

and the mihrab,
the niche in the mosque,
points the direction of prayer

actually prayer
might be going
both ways at once

the soprano singing as sorceress
turns men to stone
to wild beasts, even a wave on the shore

these arpeggios
trilling up and down

transport us.

UNSEASONABLE

snow in early autumn
in these mountains
when only a few leaves have turned

you leave a used
face mask
and a paper bag
of tomatoes
behind

how long we've lived
together, you and I
how easy—how difficult—
to part

in this
unseasonable weather.

Tashlich, 5781

in the waterless river
still there are fish
that will swallow
the crumbs of regret
I toss from the loaf

some call it sin,
the poorly done, the undone,
of these
self-hatred
is the worst

every driver's lips
are moving
in the traffic
on Cerrillos Road
in the city
of the Holy Faith
we pray in our cars
while maneuvering
angrily, carelessly
without precision
in our turns

I used to pray
let me
understand

the question—
what anyone
is actually asking of me

now I just
pray for rain.

TWIN CAMPS

I sucked in adrenaline and fear along with my mother's thin bluish milk. I weaned myself off it by biting her when I was seven months old. In her version, I continued to bite her, and to reject her. Food was ambiguous. We were forced to drink a glass of milk a day. I'd spit it out, or even vomit—slightly lacto-intolerant to this day. I weaned myself onto coffee, and then stopped drinking it for two years as an adult. My joke—I remember nothing about that time. Pour half and half into coffee until it is almost…milk.

Space surrounds me in the darkness, soft, velvet, tangible. Hypnogogic hallucinations turn the darkness into myriad sparkling dots. As a child I think I am seeing atoms or something very…real. Turns out, I'm not the only one to see neon pink anemones swell and stir in gentle ocean waves.

Even now that I'm old, when I'm alone in bed I'll hold out both hands to cup the darkness. I don't attempt to drink it because I am still on the side of the line with the village of the living, not the village of the dead. Of course both villages are identical, if mirror images of each other. Steeple, plane trees, frozen pond…there are two of each. Do you see me? A tiny figure in a red hat but only one mitten. A magpie has flown off with the knit mitten that should cover the thumb of my left hand.

I tried to live on bird seed, on words, on icicles. I tried to live on your love and glasses of tap water. I tried to live on very hot dumplings and a sense of justice. I tried to live without dipping sauce or green mustard or a sense of accomplishment. It turns out I needed air and praise.

I was forbidden to draw the twin villages and so I simply wrote down what I had seen. I told you I would never leave you, and I did not lie. I put you, small and naked, up in an apricot tree until I could tell you no longer liked that and wanted to come down. The leaves turned orange. What they covered was neither secret nor obvious, but a ground of being.

MR. DEATH

you say
"I know about
your other boyfriend
Death"

walking the arroyo
descansos
in the culvert
altars
to the abruptly
departed
—gone water

out in the desert
a windmill stock pond
full of golden koi

was I like that
when I was young?
tended or neglected?

on this lined page
a fractured narrative
I must have written
but have forgotten

in a notebook bound
in a reproduction of Courbet's
The Calm Sea

"That's Mr. Death to you."

STASIS

what you fear

you will not
necessarily find
but you will
think you see it
thrashing in the shallows

every summer
the Gulf Stream
brought pilot whales
the southern tip
of the northern lights
green horizon

dying, my mother said
she was in
"the burning place"
no Christian hell
she meant Auschwitz

I refuse
to budge from this spot
with rough-colored daisies
decorative grass
not just blue
dragonflies but

red ones too
beneath the portal
at Hope's

the tide of day
brings everything
to my door
and the outflow of darkness
touches my feet
with both kinds of worlds.

AMONG KILIMS

the weaver knots the thread
sky blue, pale red, argentine

imperial powers come again
the cost of being a land bridge

giant Buddhas in still larger caves
step forward, serene in samsara

even blown to smithereens
life still is suffering

I've made mistakes myself
and hurt your feelings when I didn't mean to

I also have a tribal name
Miriam bat Eli, if I answer to it

my lips touched the rim
my tongue sipped wine

as if a taste of this
was also a taste of the divine.

STICK CHART

it's not a map
or even a story

rather a mnemonic
for the situation of islands

the way I might trace
your face in the dark

the problem of topography
was that dreams, dissolving

flavored the day
with loss, and disorientation

of arriving at the train station
late at night

and not understanding
where Tokyo was

in the imagination
which is why

when we got off the local
in the neighborhood of food stalls

I burst into tears
seeing the full moon rise

like a whole note
on wires

I thought I was
in an Edo woodblock print

but when I looked
at my silk sleeves

I saw you'd shaved your head
and burned to ash.

SPRING IS COMING

I know that spring is coming,
desire in our always broken hearts,
chipped and mended so many times
like Japanese teacups
no longer the original color
but gold in the cracks
until the breaks predominate
and the whole cup is precious metal.

Stepping out from the black and white movie
to find the world in color
more vivid than before
or turning the pages of the book
a sudden flush of vastness.
These moments cannot
be possessed, traded for love
or a black slouch hat
but fall through the soft air
as if slipping from bare branches.
like meteors, wishes, or blossoms.

START AGAIN is set in Avenir, a twentieth century font designed
by Adrian Frutiger,
derived from the futurist fonts of the 1920s.